anythink

D0884685

SUN

Julie K. Lundgren

Rourke
Educational Media

rourkeeducationalmedia.com

Scan for Related Titles and Teacher Resources

Teaching Focus:
Vocabulary - Find the words in the book that are related to science concepts. What do these science words mean?

Before Reading:

Building Academic Vocabulary and Background Knowledge
Before reading a book, it is important to set the stage for your child or student by using pre-reading strategies. This will help them develop their vocabulary, increase their reading comprehension, and make connections across the curriculum.
1. Read the title and look at the cover. *Let's make predictions about what this book will be about.*
2. Take a picture walk by talking about the pictures/photographs in the book. Implant the vocabulary as you take the picture walk. Be sure to talk about the text features such as headings, Table of Contents, glossary, bolded words, captions, charts/diagrams, or Index.
3. Have students read the first page of text with you then have students read the remaining text.
4. Strategy Talk – use to assist students while reading.
   - Get your mouth ready
   - Look at the picture
   - Think…does it make sense
   - Think…does it look right
   - Think…does it sound right
   - Chunk it – by looking for a part you know
5. Read it again.
6. After reading the book complete the activities below.

Content Area Vocabulary
Use glossary words in a sentence.

atmosphere
gravity
orbits
satellites
solar system
sunspots

After Reading:

Comprehension and Extension Activity
After reading the book, work on the following questions with your child or students in order to check their level of reading comprehension and content mastery.
1. *Explain how sunspots are formed.* (Summarize)
2. *What are some ways you use the Sun?* (Text to self connection)
3. *What does the turning of the Earth cause?* (Summarize)
4. *What is the Sun?* (Asking questions)

Extension Activity
The Sun's rays are powerful but necessary for life on Earth. To see just how powerful they are, first find a sheet of very bright or very dark colored construction paper such as blue, purple, brown, or red. Next find objects of different sizes to place on the paper. These can be a clock, a shoe, an action figure, a doll, or a toy car. Now place the paper with the objects on it in direct sunlight for the day. What do you think will happen to the paper at the end of the day? When the Sun is down remove the objects from the paper. What do you notice? What changes have occurred?

Table of Contents

Our Nearest Star

At night, thousands of stars shine. By day, you can see just one. Earth and the other planets circle the Sun, the star in the center of our **solar system**.

Sun

Mercury

Venus

Earth

Mars

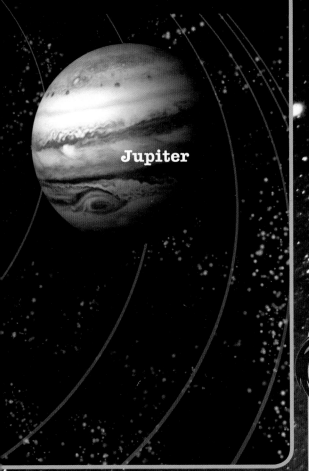

Earth is the third planet from the Sun.

Jupiter

The Sun looks much bigger than other stars because it is so much closer. Just 93 million miles (150 million kilometers) separate Earth from the Sun.

It takes about eight minutes for the Sun's light to reach Earth. The light from the next closest star takes over four years to reach Earth.

The Sun, like other stars, is a huge ball of burning gases. The Sun contains mostly hydrogen gas and some helium.

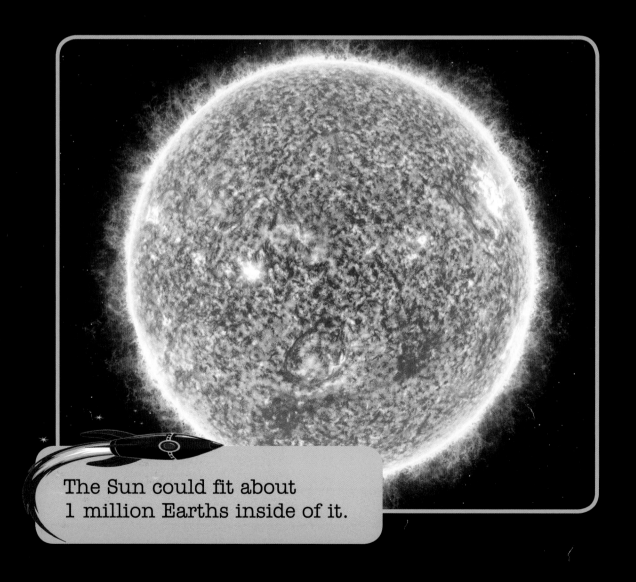

The Sun could fit about 1 million Earths inside of it.

The Sun's surface temperature is about 10,000° Fahrenheit (5,700° Celsius). The Sun has a thin **atmosphere** called the corona. The corona's temperature is nearly 200 times hotter than the Sun's surface.

During a solar eclipse, the Moon hides part or most of the Sun and we can see the corona more easily.

Eight planets revolve
around our Sun.

The Sun's great weight causes it to have strong **gravity.**

The Sun's gravity holds its gases in a ball. The Sun's gravity also holds planets in their **orbits.**

Energy Provider

The Sun's burning gases make heat and light, causing Earth's weather and climate.

The Sun bathes Earth in the right amount of heat and light to support life.

Earth has liquid water, needed for life.

Plants use sunlight to make their own food. Animals and people eat plants and other animals for energy.

The Sun formed over 4 billion years ago. It has enough energy to burn for another 5 billion years.

When you take a bite, you are eating energy that started at the Sun.

13

The Sun in Action

Just as Earth turns, so does the Sun. Our solar system also orbits the center of a group of stars and planets called the Milky Way galaxy.

The Milky Way

The Milky Way is a giant swirling spiral of millions of stars. New stars form from the space dust and gas it contains.

Our solar system lies in one arm of the Milky Way galaxy.

The Sun's gases move, swirl, and spurt. Cooler areas form dark **sunspots**. Solar flares shoot hot streams of burning gas into space.

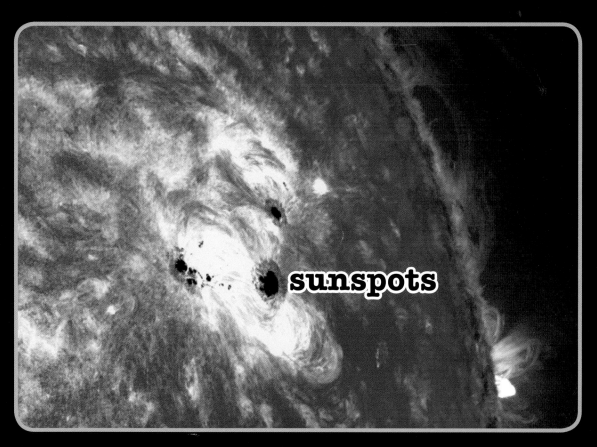

sunspots

The Sun's surface changes constantly.

When solar flares are active, we see glowing red and green lights called the aurora borealis in the winter night sky.

The Sun's movement does not cause sunrise and sunset. Instead, they happen because of the turning of the Earth.

Long ago, people believed the Sun moved around the Earth.

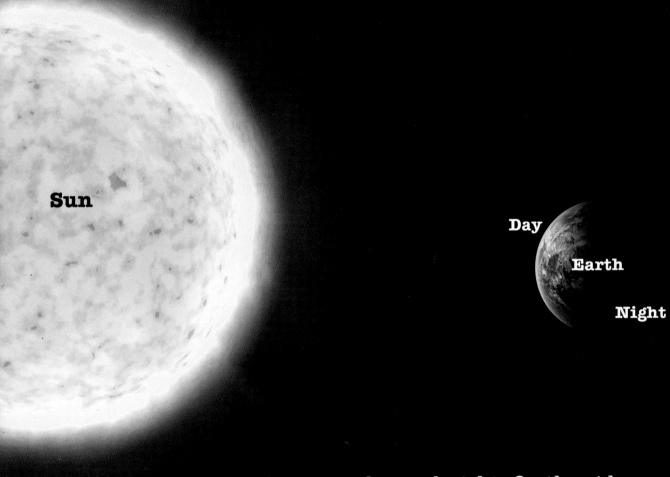

Sun

Day

Earth

Night

The spin of the Earth causes day and night. On the side of the Earth facing the Sun, it's daytime. On the side of the Earth facing away from the Sun, it's nighttime.

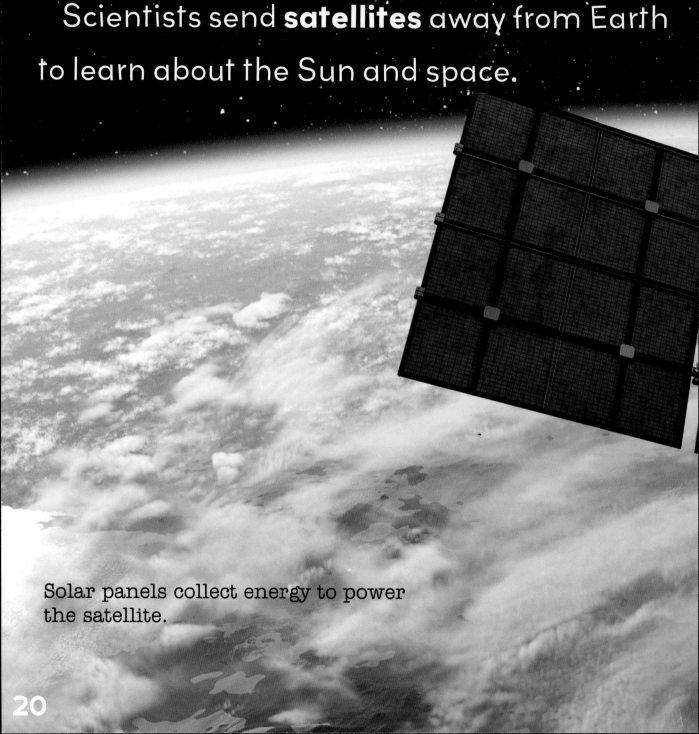

Scientists send **satellites** away from Earth to learn about the Sun and space.

Solar panels collect energy to power the satellite.

Scientists hoping to find other life in the universe look for stars and planets like ours.

satellite

Photo Glossary

atmosphere (AT-muhs-feer): This is the layer of gases surrounding a planet.

gravity (GRAV-uh-tee): This natural force pulls solids, liquids and gases to the surface of a planet or moon.

orbits (OR-bits): This describes the movement in a set path around a larger object like a planet or star.

 **satellites** (SAT-uh-lites): Any object that orbits Earth or another planet is a satellite.

 **solar system** (SOH-lur SISS-tuhm): Our solar system is the Sun and all the objects orbiting it, including planets, moons, comets, and asteroids.

 **sunspots** (SUHN-spahts): Sunspots are cooler areas that are visible on the surface of the Sun.

Index

Websites

spaceplace.nasa.gov/solar-system-formation/en/
www.nasa.gov/audience/forstudents/k-4/stories/what-is-orbit-k4.
    html#.UsnAU3m76YA
www.nasa.gov/mission_pages/sunearth/news/camilla-flight.html

Meet The Author!
www.meetREMauthors.com

About the Author

Julie K. Lundgren holds a deep fascination for plants, animals, and science about the natural environment. She gets inspiration from her beloved Minnesota, home of many large mosquitoes, muskies, and potholes.

www.rourkeeducationalmedia.com

PHOTO CREDITS: Cover and title page © Triff; Page 4-5 © Traveller Martin; Page 5 © Christos Georghiou; Page 6 © Vadim Sadovski; Page 7 © Ethan Daniels; Page 8-9 © Orla; Page 10-11 © KingJC; Page 11 © tommaso lizzul; Page 12 © Carlos Horta; Page 14-15 © MarcelClemens; Page 16-17 © Pi-Lens; Page 16 courtesy of NASA; Page 18 © Valio; inset photo © alessandro0770; Page 19 © Sebikus; Page 20-21 © Mechanik

Edited by Jill Sherman

Cover design and Interior design: Nicola Stratford   nicolastratford.com

Library of Congress PCN Data

Sun / Julie K. Lundgren
(Inside Outer Space)
ISBN 978-1-62717-726-9 (hard cover)
ISBN 978-1-62717-848-8 (soft cover)
ISBN 978-1-62717-960-7 (e-Book)
Library of Congress Control Number: 2014935651

Rourke Educational Media
Printed in the United States of America, North Mankato, Minnesota

Also Available as:
e-Books
ROURKE'S